It's all about …

DEADLY
DINOSAURS

KINGFISHER
NEW YORK

KINGFISHER
LONDON & NEW YORK

Copyright © Macmillan Publishers International Ltd 2016
Published in the United States by Kingfisher,
175 Fifth Ave., New York, NY 10010
Kingfisher is an imprint of Macmillan Children's Books, London

Distributed in the U.S. and Canada by Macmillan,
175 Fifth Ave., New York, NY 10010

Library of Congress Cataloging-in-Publication data
has been applied for.

Series editor: Sarah Snashall
Series design: Little Red Ant
Adapted from an original text by Claire Llewellyn and Thea Feldman

ISBN 978-0-7534-7261-3

Kingfisher books are available for special promotions
and premiums. For details contact: Special Markets
Department, Macmillan, 175 Fifth Ave.,
New York, NY 10010.

For more information, please visit
www.kingfisherbooks.com

Printed in China

9 8 7 6 5 4 3 2 1

1TR/1115/WKT/UG/128MA

Picture credits
The Publisher would like to thank the following for permission to reproduce their material.
Top = t; Bottom = b; Center = c; Left = l; Right = r
Pages 2–3, 6–7 & 30–31 Shutterstock/Catmando; 4bl Corbis/Corey Ford; 5cr Shutterstock/
Catmando; 22b Shutterstock/Catmando; 22-23 & 23 Shutterstock/Michael Rosskothen;
24–25 Shutterstock/sdecoret; 25 Shutterstock/miha de; 28 Shutterstock/Jorg Hackemann;
29t Shutterstock/mikeledray; 29b Shutterstock/valda.
Cards: Front bl Shutterstock/Elenarts; tr Shutterstock/Jean-Michel Girard; br Shutterstock/
Michael Rosskothen; Back tl & tr Shutterstock/Michael Rosskothen.
All other images Kingfisher Artbank.

Front cover: The deadly *Tyrannosaurus rex* hunts for prey.

CONTENTS

For your free audio download go to
www.panmacmillan.com/audio/Deadly
Dinosaurs **or** goo.gl/rFuqk3
Happy listening!

Ancient reptiles

Dinosaurs were reptiles that lived between about 230 and 65 million years ago. They were the most important land animals of their time.

FACT...

The long stretch of Earth's early history is split into three eras, or periods: Triassic, Jurassic, and Cretaceous.

Triassic era
251–200 million
years ago

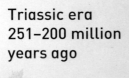

Eoraptor

Jurassic era
200–145 million
years ago

Dimorphodon

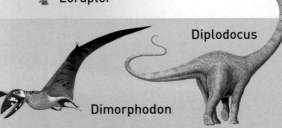

Diplodocus

Cretaceous era
145–65 million
years ago

Parasaurolophus

Deinonychus

Most dinosaurs ate plants, but some were the deadliest meat eaters the world has ever seen. Some dinosaurs were as long as three houses; others were the size of a chicken..

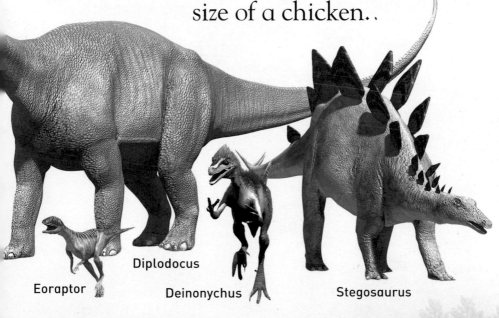

Diplodocus

Eoraptor

Deinonychus

Stegosaurus

Stegosaurus

Allosaurus

Maiasaura

Tyrannosaurus rex

Gentle giant

Diplodocus was huge! It had a big body, strong legs, a long neck and tail, but its head was small.

FACT ...

Diplodocus swallowed stones to help crush the food in its stomach.

Ferns were food for Diplodocus and other plant eaters.

Diplodocus fed on bushes and trees, tearing off leaves with its teeth. Diplodocus was so massive that it had to eat all the time just to stay alive.

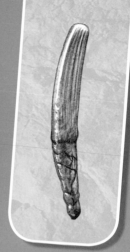

Diplodocus had teeth like this.

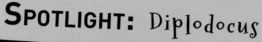

SPOTLIGHT: Diplodocus

Size:	up to 115 ft. (35m) long
Habitat:	close to rivers
Food:	moss, ferns, and trees
Lived:	155–145 million years ago

Killing machine

Allosaurus was an excellent hunter. It was one of the deadliest killers of all time.

Allosaurus teeth had zigzag edges to saw through flesh.

Allosaurus stood on its strong back legs and ran very fast after its prey. It had big jaws, sharp teeth, and long claws to strip the meat from its victim.

SPOTLIGHT: Allosaurus

Size:	up to 40 ft. (12m) long
Habitat:	grasslands and forest
Food:	other dinosaurs
Lived:	155–144 million years ago

Armor-plated dinosaur

Stegosaurus was like a walking tank. It was about the same size as Allosaurus but it walked on four legs. It had bony studs to protect its neck, hard plates along its back, and spines on its tail.

Stegosaurus ate plants, so it did not need sharp teeth or claws. If a meat eater attacked, Stegosaurus swung its tail and smashed the hunter with its spines!

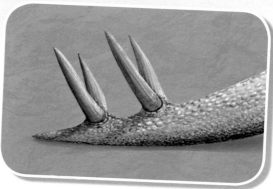

Stegosaurus had sharp spines on its tail.

SPOTLIGHT: Stegosaurus

Size: about 30 ft. (9m) long, 13 ft. (4m) tall

Habitat: woods

Food: moss, ferns, conifers

Lived: 156–140 million years ago

Flying reptiles

Dinosaurs could not fly but there were massive flying reptiles called pterosaurs at the time of the dinosaurs.

Spotlight: Dimorphodon

Size: 3 ft. (1m) long, 5 ft. (1.5m) wingspan
Habitat: near coasts
Food: insects and fish
Lived: 197–195 million years ago

Pterosaurs had wings made of skin and
were the first bony animals to fly.
A pterosaur caught insects in its mouth
as it flew through the air.

Dimorphodon was a pterosaur
with many sharp teeth.

Duckbill dinosaurs

Duckbill dinosaurs were plant-eating
dinosaurs. They lived in herds near rivers.
The dinosaurs called to each other with
booms, honks, or squeaks.

Parasaurolophus

The crests of duckbill dinosaurs came in different colors and shapes.

FACT ...

Each herd had a different crest on their heads and a different skin pattern, too.

SPOTLIGHT: Parasaurolophus

Size:	about 33 ft. (10m) long
Habitat:	rivers, lakes, and coasts
Food:	pine needles, leaves, twigs, and ferns
Lived:	76–65 million years ago

15

Baby duckbills

Most (maybe all) dinosaurs laid eggs.
Duckbill dinosaurs called Maiasaura
made their nests in the sand by
rivers and lakes.

Baby Maiasaura were very small when they hatched. When they were big enough to walk, the herd would leave the sandy beach to look for food. The herd would return to the same beach to lay eggs the next year.

Maiasaura egg

SPOTLIGHT: Maiasaura

Size:	about 30 ft. (9m) long
Habitat:	by rivers and lakes
Food:	leaves, berries, seeds, and ferns
Lived:	80–65 million years ago

Terrible claws!

Deinonychus was a dangerous meat eater with sharp curving teeth. It had claws on its hands and feet. One special claw on each foot was long and curved to cut and slash its prey.

SPOTLIGHT: Deinonychus

Size:	up to 10 ft. (3m) long
Habitat:	swamps and forests
Food:	meat
Lived:	115–108 million years ago

Deinonychus were fast runners and hunted in packs. Together, they killed big duckbills and other plant eating dinosaurs.

Deinonychus's curved claw was five inches (13 centimeters) long!

A pack of Deinonychus attack a big plant eater.

The king

Tyrannosaurus rex was one of the biggest meat eaters of its time. It had a massive head and strong jaws that could crush bone.

Tyrannosaurus rex had big, powerful legs and could run very fast, but it had very small arms. It would track its prey, then charge at it and grab it in its jaws.

Size: about 40 ft. (12m) long
Habitat: warm forests, near rivers and swamps
Food: meat
Lived: 85–65 million years ago

FACT ...

The tooth of a Tyrannosaurus rex has been found buried in the back of a plant-eating Hadrosaur.

This Tyrannosaurus rex tooth is 12 in. (30 centimeters) long.

Sea monsters

Dinosaurs lived on land, but at the same time vast sea monsters swam in the ocean.

Megalodon was a prehistoric shark three times bigger than a great white shark. Liopleurodon was a reptile with 10-feet-long (three-meter-long) jaws.

Liopleurodon

Megalodon

Sarcosuchus was the largest crocodile ever.

FACT ...

Sharks lived in the oceans for millions of years before the dinosaurs—and for millions of years afterward.

The end

Dinosaurs lived on Earth until they suddenly died out over 65 million years ago. At that time, something terrible happened to Earth that wiped out all of the dinosaurs, pterosaurs, and large ocean reptiles. Most scientists believe that a large asteroid hit Earth. It created dust and huge floods that covered the whole planet.

When the asteroid hit, so much dust went up into the sky that it was winter for many years on Earth.

Morganucodon is an early mammal that lived during the late Triassic period.

FACT ...

Small animals survived the asteroid event. When the dinosaurs died out, mammals and birds took over Earth.

Dinosaur hunt

Although dinosaurs are extinct we find out about them from the fossils that are left behind.

These scientists have found a fossilized dinosaur.

Fossils are made over millions of years.
The remains of a dinosaur are buried,
and sand and mud press down on them.
The spaces where the bones were fill
with minerals and become rocks in the
shape of bones—we call these fossils.

A dinosaur dies by a river. It becomes covered with mud and sand.

The sand and mud protect the remains from the wind and weather. The remains become fossils.

The rock made from sand and mud is worn away by wind and water. The fossils can now be seen.

At the museum

Sometimes scientists find a complete dinosaur skeleton. The skeleton shows the size of an animal, what it looked like, and what it ate. It does not show what color it was or what sounds it made.

This Tyrannosaurus rex skeleton is in the American Museum of Natural History.

Scientists have found fossilized dinosaur footprints. These footprints show how an animal stood and moved. They show if it lived alone or with others in a herd.

a fossilized dinosaur footprint

You can see the bony plates along the back of this Stegosaurus skeleton.

GLOSSARY

asteroid A piece of rock from space.

conifer A tree that grows cones such as a pine tree.

era A period of time in the past.

extinct No longer living on Earth.

fern A green plant that has no flowers.

fossil A part of a plant or animal that has turned to stone.

herd A group of animals that live together.

minerals Rock like substances that are dissolved in water. Minerals replace the bones of a dinosaur to make fossils.

pack A group of animals that hunt together.

plate A hard, flat bit of horn or bone that protects an animal's body.

prey Animals hunted by others for food.

pterosaur A flying reptile that lived at the same time as dinosaurs.

reptile A cold-blooded animal with bones, which often has scales and lays eggs.

spine A sharp, pointed bit of horn or bone.

stud A small, hard bit of horn or bone.

swamp A boggy area.